# 64 Part 2
## Nikey Pasco-Dunston

WITHDRAWN

S0-ASC-340

*64 Collected Thoughts That*
*Will Make You Think*

# PART 2

BROUGHT TO YOU BY:
NIKEY PASCO-DUNSTON

64 Part 2
Nikey Pasco-Dunston

710 EMG Publishing
P.O Box 71
Villa Rica, GA 30180

Copyright © 2017 by Nikey Pasco-Dunston

All rights reserved. No parts of this book may be reproduced in any form or by any means without the prior written consent of the Publisher, except brief quotes used in reviews.

If you purchased this book without a cover, you should be aware that this is stolen property. It was reported as "unsold and destroyed" to the Publisher and neither the Author nor the Publisher has received any payment for this "stripped book."

Cover by Melarts Marketing Solutions (Nigeria)
Editing by Editor-In-Chief of 710 Publishing, Nikey Pasco-Dunston.

710 Publishing Titles, Imprints, and Distributed Lines may be purchased at exclusive quantity discounts for bulk orders for fund-raising, educational/institutional use, and special sales promotions. For more information, contact the publisher, 710 Publishing, at:
WePublish@710Entertainment.com

Printed in the United States of America

64 Part 2
Nikey Pasco-Dunston

Disclaimer: The chapters inside of this book are not directed toward one specific person or situation.

Confession: This book has everything to do with my life and life in general. Wisdom and knowledge should be present before propagation and that is what I deem.

Secret: I cried writing parts of this book.

Dedication: I dedicate this title to everyone out there in need of love, encouragement, and uplifting. I've been in your same predicament before and I know how it feels to need a boost of positivity. 64 Part 1 and Part 2 will do it for you – enjoy!

## *What's Inside...*

## Why 64?

You may be wondering why did I name this book 64? Well, that answer is very simple. The numbers 6 and 4 are positive numbers and when their properties and energies are combined-together they become dynamic!

The number 6 transfers frequencies of gratitude, grace, simplicity, domestication, service to others, guardianship, responsibility, and the monetary and material aspects of life. The number 4 adds in its frequencies of feasibility, progression, production, management, building solid foundations for others and yourself, willpower, loyalty, and inner-wisdom.

The number 64 signifies that every bit of the effort and hard work that you put into your aspirations will have long-term blessings for you and your loved ones. No matter what obstacle you come across do not give up because you will achieve your goals just continue to work hard. Remain positive about your materialistic and financial problems because the universe's energy is taken care of those areas as you read this.

Through my studies, I learned that the number 64 delivers such powerful energy that it gives one the ability to see themselves in a higher light. It is a true self-esteem booster. 64 is a very powerful number and this book will bring out that energy to whoever reads it. So, continue to read through '64' and take in the positive energy that I release through each one of my 64 motivational quotes and my short lectures.

## 64 IS GUARANTEED TO MOVE YOU!

## Life & Love
### (Love Sometimes Means Pain)

I overheard an older woman (widow) telling a younger woman that it's always good to have another man on the side because men find every excuse to be a dog and treat a woman wrong. No matter how good a woman is to a man - he'll find every reason to treat her like a bitch. She said: "Treat that nigga the same way he is treating you...TEN-FOLD!" I did not interrupt...I just listened to her thoughts and beliefs on marriage and relationships and I let it all soak in.

Not all advice is good advice but it's always good to listen to other people's opinions. Which brings me to this:
If that woman does what the older woman said then society will automatically label her a hoe or thot but when a man does that there's nothing wrong. Most of the time he is getting praised for being a nasty nicca. "YOU DA MAN, YOU DA MAN!" Type of praise.

I say, do as you please. If you want to get even by seeing another man then do it but to me, the sweetest revenge is LEAVING. Just walk away and take everything you had to offer with you when you leave. Trust and believe that will hurt him the most and he will regret every foul decision he made. Don't risk damaging your temple (insides) for a quick thrill or payback. There are too many diseases and crazy people in this world for that kind of nonsense. Be smarter than most and just leave that painful situation where it stands.

A lot of times the flame and infatuation in a relationship will burn out. That blazing hot flame could last as-long-as four or five years and suddenly, right before your eyes, POOF -- it's gone. Then before you realize it you are the only one fighting to reignite that flame. You realize or begin to believe that maybe your significant other never loved you like they claimed they did due to their actions and lack of betterment. Maybe that is not the case but then again, maybe it is. Sure, you are going to cry; let it all out. Sure, you may feel like screaming; let that out too. But one thing that I advise you to do is not to allow yourself to slip into a deep depression because I'm telling you that it's not worth it.

It does not matter what your situation is hence there is someone out there that will wholly appreciate you and everything that comes with you with open arms. If you know that you are a good woman or man, then that is all more of a reason for you not to keep fighting for a relationship when your partner could care less about the fight. If your significant other refuses to genuinely love you back and is not giving you their one hundred percent – the percentage is high that he or she is focused on someone or something else.

Trust and believe they will learn that their decision was not the best and they will regret it losing you. Now, that is completely up to your discretion to accept them back into your life or not. But before you do so, think about YOU first - don't suddenly catch amnesia.

They want to be free and do as they please?
They refuse to give you their all and commit to you?

When you don't ask for much but when you do finally ask for something and you can't even receive the little you asked for - you will begin to question everything. Just follow your instinct... Do yourself that favor and LET THEM GO!

You deserve so much more. Your life and feelings are not meant to be strung along like you're some kind of Muppet. Regain your control and cut those strings! We all have problems but it's all about how we solve them. That's what matters the most. So, just take things one day at a time and take notes while you're at it. Life is too short to be rushed, thrown away, or wasted. So, enjoy it while it lasts!

## 64 Part 2
### Nikey Pasco-Dunston

Below are some quotes of mine that came to my mind as I directed my thoughts in on the pain that can be found deep inside of love.

~~~~~

To love and appreciate are verbs. You must show it in order for it to be recognized and returned.
- Nikey Pasco-Dunston

If you truly appreciate someone then let them know how you feel. A silent mouth & no actions are as good as dead.
- Nikey Pasco-Dunston

Tell her that you love her and that she's beautiful every day and watch how much love she gives you in return.
- Nikey Pasco-Dunston

Love should flow out easily like water and not be forced out like oil in the earth.
- Nikey Pasco-Dunston

You know what you deserve. You deserve limitless love, respect, and everlasting peace.
- Nikey Pasco-Dunston

Now I will switch that up for you. That right there was my original quote and on the next page I re-worded it just for you.

I know what I deserve and that's limitless love, respect, and everlasting peace.
- Nikey Pasco-Dunston

If you love someone make sure that you tell them you love them EVERY DAY and you need to SHOW IT too.
- Nikey Pasco-Dunston

If you need someone then make sure that they know it. They'll never know unless you make it known.
- Nikey Pasco-Dunston

Sometimes it's best to keep the space and just love them from a distance. Not everyone belongs in your life.
- Nikey Pasco-Dunston

Not everyone deserves all of YOU. If they don't appreciate what you have to offer, then don't ever offer it again.
- Nikey Pasco-Dunston

True love doesn't die - it only grows stronger. Infatuations and rebounds die off shortly after the heart finds something or someone else of interest.
- Nikey Pasco-Dunston

Heartbreak is something that we all face at one point in our lives but the key to the pain is the lesson behind it. It's all a learning experience.

## Life & Pain

Sometimes it's best to leave. Forget what people think...follow your heart and JUST MOVE ON. There is nothing worse than repeating the same song that makes you weep and causes you to lose sleep. Stop the tape and play something that will bring back that euphoric feeling into your life again. Believe me, you will not regret it.

~~~~~

It's dangerous to hold on to something that is not secure on the other end. Don't hurt yourself -- Just let it go.
- Nikey Pasco-Dunston

Pain is not always a terrible thing. At least now your third eye is more open and you were taught a valuable lesson.
- Nikey Pasco-Dunston

Don't feel bad for me -- feel bad for the soul that hurt me.
- Nikey Pasco-Dunston

If your hope & faith ran dry, would you let it go or dig deep for more? Sometimes it is best to just let it go.
- Nikey Pasco-Dunston

## 64 Part 2
### Nikey Pasco-Dunston

A dose of your own medicine might make you pass out. Watch how you treat people.
- Nikey Pasco-Dunston

I was in pain because I believed in what I was told but once I learned that I was deceived...I felt bad for the fool that lied.

# Life & Self

Your "flaws" are beauty marks that you fail to recognize due to the standards of society. Never let the opinions of others convince you otherwise. You were distinctively created to be the extraordinary person you are today. Never forget these words because what I say is the truth.

You are LIFE so let your positive energy flow and drift in the air like the wind. Choose not to dwell on anything negative that you can't change because it only hinders your mental growth process. Remember that it is your choice; you control your thoughts and feelings – no one else but you. If you don't truly love yourself how are you going to love anyone else? How could you possibly be friends with anyone else if you are not a friend to yourself first? It is time for you to make yourself "Head of Self" because if you continue to allow someone else to claim your mind and run your life then you will never know your worth. You must love yourself. ♀

~~~~~

As much as you may not want to say "no" that is what you need to do. It's time to focus on YOU!
- Nikey Pasco-Dunston

I felt rejuvenated once I stopped helping ungrateful people. Ingrate people must learn the hard way.
- Nikey Pasco-Dunston

There's always someone that looks for the negative in a positive. Use that as fuel to go even harder at whatever it is you're doing.
- Nikey Pasco-Dunston

Never let the jealousy of others distract you from accomplishing your goals. You are stronger than that. Stay focused!
- Nikey Pasco-Dunston

The power to move forward is within you! Don't give up.
- Nikey Pasco-Dunston

Choose not to dwell on anything negative that you can't change because it only hinders your mental growth process.
- Nikey Pasco-Dunston

Never let a negative moment ruin your entire day. Life is too short to waste on such a temporary emotion.
- Nikey Pasco-Dunston

Nothing is permanent except for the past but you do not have to live there. Create new memories. Leave the past where it's at.
- Nikey Pasco-Dunston

When nothing goes as planned - toss the agenda and start anew. There's nothing better than a fresh new start.
- Nikey Pasco-Dunston

What I love about a new day is being able to start anew. Focus on your vision because everything else is a distraction.
- Nikey Pasco-Dunston

What's most important is having a better day than yesterday because you can never get today back.
- Nikey Pasco-Dunston

If the objective is to be stress-free and at peace, then don't make things more difficult than they should be.
- Nikey Pasco-Dunston

You must think positive if you want to get positive results. Nothing good happens for a person with a negative mind.
- Nikey Pasco-Dunston

I'm always perfecting my imperfections until they are perfect. Since nothing is perfect, I'm always working and learning new things.
- Nikey Pasco-Dunston

Learn to look within yourself for answers. We all go through storms but you have to be strong enough to

make it out in one piece.
- Nikey Pasco-Dunston

Sometimes you need to look at yourself and call on the inner God within you. Usually, that's all it takes.
- Nikey Pasco-Dunston

There will only be one you on this earth and that right there should tell you how special you are. Don't you ever underestimate the power within you!

## Life & Success

Many nights I stay up late working on accomplishing my biggest dreams and I might even fall asleep on my laptop. With only a few hours of sleep, I still wake up early because I have a vision of success that will soon bring me ultimate peace. I don't wake up searching the internet to see what is trending in the entertainment world. I don't wake up searching the internet wondering what new sneakers are about to hit the market so I can get them first. I don't wake up scrolling my social media timelines to see "What's on someone else's mind" because I do not care about anything of that; especially moments after I first open my eyes.

The first thing on my mind when I open my eyes is "Work harder so your family won't ever have to struggle again" and at that very moment, I grab my laptop and get to business. I stopped working on building someone else's dream years ago, and that was my choice. I chose to work even harder at building my own dream and I never looked back in regret.

Being an entrepreneur is not always peaches and cream like a lot of outsiders looking in think that is. It takes a great deal of hard work, dedication, investments, and sometimes even tears just to make ends meet. It takes an abundance of patience, knowledge, and the willingness to learn to make it out here in this savage business world.

Becoming your own boss is not always the easiest thing to be but it has great advantages and one of the main advantages that keeps me going is the fact that as-long-as-I continue to work hard, that in due time, everything that I invested in will pay off and I will be at peace.

No matter what anyone says to you about how crazy you are for thinking outside of their box, keep thinking like a boss and you will, in fact, become THAT BOSS!

NEVER GIVE UP.

NEVER SETTLE FOR LESS.

NEVER FOLD UNDER PRESSURE.

Those are the three affirmations that I tell myself daily except I say "I WILL NOT GIVE UP. I WILL NOT SETTLE FOR LESS. I WILL NOT FOLD UNDER PRESSURE." I slowly inhale and then I slowly exhale and repeat those affirmations several times before I start my day. Pay no mind to the nasty negative critics because they are not paying you. Keep your eyes on your vision and don't lose focus because your time is coming. So, don't give up!

~~~~~

Not everyone has the same vision as you or believes in your dream until they see your dream come true. Then everyone believes in you!
- Nikey Pasco-Dunston

Greatness is learning something new, valuable, and priceless every day. That should be a part of everyone's daily goal.
- Nikey Pasco-Dunston

A successful person is a person that is always eager to learn something new.
- Nikey Pasco-Dunston

A successful person understands the importance of constant education. Every day you should want to learn something new.
- Nikey Pasco-Dunston

A successful person listens more than they speak and they also pay attention to detail.
- Nikey Pasco-Dunston

Take full advantage of all the opportunities presented to you - but don't abuse them. You might need to go that route again.
- Nikey Pasco-Dunston

If you believe in yourself then invest in yourself. There's no half stepping to success.
- Nikey Pasco-Dunston

Faith should be your best friend. Whatever you do, don't lose hope and continue to work hard. Keep the faith.
- Nikey Pasco-Dunston

Don't care about other's supporting you, as-long-as YOU support YOU that is all that counts. People will see your passion and eventually follow suit.
- Nikey Pasco-Dunston

In the world that we live in today, how could you not think about being successful? Everyone has their own perspective and light on success so don't let someone else's light out shine yours. Never give up on your hopes, dreams, and aspirations.

# Life & General Thoughts

When I think about the meaning behind my dreams, I start to really focus in on reality. My mission is nowhere near complete...there's so much more in this world for me to see and do. Which brings me to my general thoughts about life...

~~~~~

I choose to keep my mind open by curiosity because there's nothing worse than believing a lie.
- Nikey Pasco-Dunston

Every woman should have high heels, high hopes, high aspirations...oh, and a pair of Adidas in her closet.
- Nikey Pasco-Dunston

When you love what you do, it becomes habitual; especially when money is involved.
- Nikey Pasco-Dunston

If you give up, then you will never know if you could have achieved your goal and completed the mission.
- Nikey Pasco-Dunston

Being blessed and at peace is extraordinary. So, don't forget to give thanks before you officially start your day.
- Nikey Pasco-Dunston

Blessed is waking up another day. Peace is what you make life out to be. It's your life -- what do you choose?
- Nikey Pasco-Dunston

QUALITY over QUANTITY! It's not always about the bars/count. Edit your work and edit it right. Think before you release!
- Nikey Pasco-Dunston

Say "thank you" to the enemy and mean it. Knowing who your enemy is, beats not knowing them at all. It's much safer.
- Nikey Pasco-Dunston

The more blessings you give, the more blessings you get back. Take note and remember that!
- Nikey Pasco-Dunston

If you can do it, then do it, and don't expect anything in return. Learn to give without recognition and shine.
- Nikey Pasco-Dunston

Be a blessing to someone else and in due time watch the blessings that will rain on you!
- Nikey Pasco-Dunston

Everything you say, think, and write can and will manifest. Be careful because you are in control.
- Nikey Pasco-Dunston

Sprinkle water on me, I'm dumping a bucket on you.
Throw a pebble at me, I'll shoot a missile at you. I
will go the extra mile!
- Nikey Pasco-Dunston

"Treat other's how you want to be treated" is an old
saying that many people turn a deaf ear to until the
shoe is on the other foot. Then they hoot and holler
about how things are not fair and how so-and-so did
them wrong. Understand and never forget that it
pays more to be kind.

Life, in general, is full of surprises so don't be
surprised when something unexpected happens; be
prepared to face it head on whether it's good or
bad. This is the life that we live so don't be scared to
live your life to the fullest.

# Life & Unity

The significance of unity is essential to our everyday livelihood. That brotherly and sisterly bond is in desperate need of restoral. Without it…everything that our ancestors ever hoped, dreamed, and fought for will continue to go down the drain. Restoring our love and respect for one another is a start to making America great again; not fighting, killing, and intentionally harming one another. That cannot be what life is about -- it can't be!

Far too often I walk in stores or even down the street and I see people looking at each other up and down, mean mugging. Their faces are all scrunched up like they just smelt something horrific. They give each other the ugliest looks as if that person took the last chocolate milk in grade school and they never got over it. I wonder if it hurts those people to be kind? A simple smile is a start to a possible new friendship or more. The worst thing is that your own flesh and blood can be the same way toward one another. It's almost like they have a point to prove to absolutely no one. Unity is more important than most people think. Unify or die trying…

~~~~~

We are more powerful as one and if we actually come together and STAY TOGETHER -- so much more will be accomplished.
- Nikey Pasco-Dunston

Less drama, more unity. We are greater together and that's a fact. You should value your people as well as your time.
- Nikey Pasco-Dunston

## Life & Energy

As young children, many of us never took a moment out of our busy days to appreciate life and it's many blessings before our eyes. It is not that we were spoiled and ungrateful; it was that we were blessed children that were blinded to the deeper perspectives of life.

Most children don't have a thought in the world of losing someone they love to someone else or even deeper – to death. You may have been sheltered from massive heartaches to preserve your innocence and childhood. That usually happens when someone loves you so much that they want to protect you from all harm.

As a parent, I believe that it's for the better of our children to talk to them about the pain they can endure from losing someone that they love. You do not have to get into specifics on certain subjects but do get into enough detail that they understand that life is not always "fair" and will not always go as expected.

Expect the unexpected.

As we age, we come to realization that nothing physical lasts forever, yet there is a multitude of people around the world convinced that the unendurable anguish and despondency will never fade away but that is not necessarily true. As time passes, the grief that you are or were feeling will eventually weaken as your heart slowly mends.

What many people fail to realize is - if it wasn't for energy, they would not feel the pain of losing someone or something that they love. That is what you call a divine connection. Without that unearthly parallelism, we would not ever feel the pain. We are godly beings with supernatural abilities that are indeed metaphysical.

That brings me to love and everlasting life. When the love is as solid as the concrete that you walk on, it won't ever completely diminish. The love and life will remain in the energy that surrounds you until the day that you transition into the afterlife and join the love that you've been missing. Now, that is if you believe in afterlife. Even if you do not believe in life after death, everlasting life takes place in energy and that is without a shadow of doubt.

Energy does not die; it only transforms into another form of existence. It is in the air that we breathe and even the water that we drink. Energy is an everlasting thing, and as-long-as you live you will feel the energy from that dear person that physically left you, especially if the feeling of love was mutual and the loss was out of the other persons' control. In due time, you will look back at the wonderful memories that you shared with them and smile.

There is no deadline to healing simply because that form of action takes time. We are unique individuals and that means that no two persons are alike – not even identical twins are completely alike. Be easy on yourself or whoever it is that is in the stage of healing. Do not ever rush that process...

~~~~~

They say life is short and that is very much true. So, don't take advantage of your blessings.
- Nikey Pasco-Dunston

Anything can happen at any given time so plan and be prepared for the future.
- Nikey Pasco-Dunston

You never know how, when, or if you might lose that special someone. So, cherish them while you have them.
- Nikey Pasco-Dunston

Losing someone you love to death is difficult to deal with but remember only a selfish soul would want you to mourn forever.
- Nikey Pasco-Dunston

There's no timeframe or special approach on bereavement. Mending a torn heart isn't a quick process so take your time.
- Nikey Pasco-Dunston

Love me while I'm physically alive because once my physical is gone my soul and spirit will be with you, forever.
- Nikey Pasco-Dunston

I believe that energy is everlasting. Here it is over 200 thousand years after my ancestors lived and I feel them to this day.
- Nikey

We are never truly dead once we "die" because our energy shifts into another dimension. We are timeless beings.
- Nikey Pasco-Dunston

## Important Contacts
~~~~~

Grief Recovery Hotline – 800-445-4808

NDMDA Depression Hotline (National Depressive &
Manic Depressive Association)

– 800-826-3632

U.S Suicide Hotline – 800-784-2433

Suicide Prevention Services Depression Hotline

– 630-482-9696

Urgent Emotional Healing & Stress Management

– 404-666-2795

# DON'T HESITATE TO SEEK HELP – YOUR HEALTH MATTERS!

# Who is Nikey Pasco-Dunston?

Nikey Pasco-Dunston, is a Boston, Massachusetts, native and she is now a resident of Atlanta, Georgia. She is a mother, author, poet, entertainer, motivational speaker, and a certified Life Coach.

Nikey has a genuine love for helping other people uplift their spirits, energy, and self-esteem. She feels like the world would be a greater place with more positive energy and happier relationships. And to her, happiness is her idea of success.

Nikey's career as an all-around entertainer and businesswoman has been recognized by many notable sources.

For Booking Contact:

info@710Entertainment.com

To Order Books Contact:

WePublish@710Entertainment.com


Facebook: @OnlyNikeyPasco

Twitter: @NikeyPasco

Instagram: @NikeyPasco

## **More Books!**

If you like 64 Part 2, then you are sure to enjoy 64 (part 1) and Scars: Steps To Queenism.

True Story & Self-Help

For Fictional & Poetic Books by Nikey Pasco-Dunston, visit her website below:

www.nikeypasco.com

46035132R00021

Made in the USA
San Bernardino, CA
24 February 2017